Homeward Bound

A collection of poems

by

Freda Weaver

Homeward Bound
An Epic Press Book
Copyright © Freda Weaver MMIX

Front Cover: The Picture shown is from a painting by the Author entitled The Delectable Mountains inspired by John Bunyon's Pilgrim's Progress. The title of the book is inspired by the same source.

Further copies can be obtained by writing to:
    Tytherington Family Worship Church,
    Sandwich Drive,
    Tytherington,
     Macclesfield,
    Cheshire.
    SK10 2UD
    Tel. 01625 615195
    Email: office@tfwchurch.org

ISBN 978-1-906557-06-5

Foreword

I feel tempted to call this book "Three Times Three makes Three" because 3 appears frequently in the Bible and this is a three-way production.

God gave me an idea, theme, a command, two or more lines of rhyme and the ability to do the job.

My part was to work out the idea, theme etc., find out where the lines fitted in and of course to make the poem rhyme and flow.

Alan's was to arrange the layout, design an attractive cover that would draw attention to the book and arrange its publication.

God's part is obvious: He has gifted the talent for me to write the poems and the skills for Alan to bring them together in this book.

My thanks are also three-way: to God, to Alan and to you for buying the book. All the proceeds will go to the Missionaries supported by Tytherington Family Worship Church in Macclesfield.

Freda Weaver

Acknowledgements
Grateful thanks to Alan Batchelor for his patience, guidance and expertise in drawing these poems together into an acceptable form for publishing. My thanks, too, to Margaret Bird for her invaluable help with spelling, punctuation, proof reading etc. as I am unable to see the printed work.

Homeward Bound

Contents

SOMETHING MISSING

I went to college on a Creative Writing course in 1999. My tutor corrected my work because I was blind. That Christmas, I was surprised when she said the rest of the class, none of whom I had met, had invited me to join them for their Christmas meal, adding that they were writing a Christmas poem which they would read out. I saw a golden opportunity to make mine a gospel one, which I recited. In the first part, I attracted their interest by describing the party, then neatly switched to the Christmas message before they were aware of what was coming. For the millennium Christmas, I had my Christmas cards professionally made with that poem inside and it evoked many letters and phone calls of appreciation.

That Christmas Day dawned bright and clear,
Again, it was that time of year.
Hollyberries and mistletoe,
Christmas tree, fairy lights aglow.

I'd made the cake and mince pies too,
I hoped the turkey was cooked through.
In each cracker, a paper hat,
I did put out the Welcome mat.

I'd sent my friends a card to say,
"Please come to tea on Christmas Day,
I have prepared a treat so rare,
Please write to say that you'll be there."

After Grace, all sat down to dine
And some they had a glass of wine.
Turkey, salad, then Christmas cake,
They loved the mince pies, my own bake.

The party went with such a swing,
Opened presents, left loads of string.
Then amid a game of wishing,
I realised - something missing.

I pondered long, what could it be
I had forgotten? Silly me.
We then all heard the Church bells chime,
And I remembered - just in time!

We'd enjoyed the celebration,
All had come by invitation.
Jesus was - I now saw the light -
The only one with no invite!

God sent Jesus on Christmas Day,
Then on the cross our debt to pay.
So one day, we can enter Heaven,
Washed and cleansed, our sins forgiven.

God too prepares a feast so rare,
He wants us all to join Him there.
Around the world, each one MUST choose,
Accept with thanks - or else refuse.

My friends agreed, I'm glad to say,
That we should all kneel down and pray.
First, asked the Lord to heal our pride,
Forgive our sins, come live inside.

We all have been so different since,
For we no longer moan or wince.
See others in a brand new way.
Now every day is Christmas Day.

Christmas 2000

CHRISTMAS TIME

These days people seem to have forgotten what Christmas is really about and I wanted to remind them of its true meaning with this poem. Darren read it out on 'Canalside Radio' just before Christmas, 2007. The Presenter added that he agreed with it. I hope that it helped at least, some listeners to remember or realise for the first time, the real meaning of Christmas. (I have a short article on the same theme, entitled Christmas Gifts.)

Say, what is your view of Christmas, what do you see?
Tinsel; crackers; fairy lights on a Christmas tree.
Enjoy the turkey; cake; mince pies and Christmas pud,
Then celebrate by drinking far more than you should?

You have to buy presents for friends and family,
Strong boots for Uncle Joe, a phone for Auntie Bee.
You are short of cash, pay by visa at the tills,
Quite forget to wonder HOW you will pay those bills.

"Merry Christmas, Happy New year," is what you call
To everyone you meet in the new market hall.
Then, when Christmas is over and has gone once more,
Will you still speak to that blind man who lives next door?

Do milling crowds frustrate till you can take no more
Of the razamataz, think Christmas is such a bore?
Will you be glad when Yuletide is over and gone,
So you can forget about it, 'til the next one?

Or, have you another view of our Christmas Day?
A Manger; a Babe in a nativity play?
Think Christmas is just for children and that is all.
Do you know who the Babe was? Do you care at all?

Have you ever wondered WHY we have Christmas Day?
Why it is so special, in such a special way?
WHY we give presents to our friends and family,
Listen while I tell you what Christmas means to me.

The Babe is the Son of God. Jesus is His name.
Since he grew to manhood, world wide has been his fame.
He had a Destiny and one He must fulfil:
Destiny with a cross, on top of Calvary's hill.

The Pharisees hated him, said that he must die,
So, nailed him on a cross that pointed to the sky.
Suffering in agony, that's how Jesus died.
"He WAS the Son of God," a Roman soldier cried.

"If he WAS the Son of God," do I hear you say,
"What crime did he commit, that he should have to pay?"
No crime, he had never sinned or spoken one lie,
'Twas to pay for our sins, that Jesus CHOSE to die.

Death could not hold God's Son, nor keep him in the tomb.
He walked right out of it, dispelling fear and gloom.
Offers us salvation, Free Pardon for our sin.
Now, opens heaven's door, invites us to come in.

God will never force us. He gave Free will, you see,
To choose down here, where our eternal home will be.
Either Heaven or Hell, for there are only two.
I have chosen heaven and pray that you will too.

This is how I view Christmas, hope I made it clear
Why Christmas is a special, special time of year.
Without Christmas; the Babe; a manger and some hay,
There'd be no Calvary, no glad Easter Day!

How do YOU view Christmas now, will you think a lot?
Take Christ out of Christmas; tell me, what have you got?
Let God's love and mercy, cleanse you from sin today,
Then, next Christmas will be YOUR very SPECIAL day.

2007

CALVARY

This poem was one of my earliest poems,which was written prior to one Easter. I was thinking about the cross and what Jesus suffered, so decided to describe the event in my own words. Originally, it was entitled "From Gory to Glory." However, when different Churches kindly included this poem in their magazine, they assumed that I had accidentally omitted an l, in the word gory, so without checking with me, they put one in. This ruined what I had intended to imply, so I changed it to "Calvary."

The cross was not a pretty sight.
For three long hours, day turned to night
While Jesus a fierce battle fought
And Satan's power crushed to nought.

Hours before, in Gethsemane
He changed the course of history.
Agonised, till the ground was wet
With pool of blood, that oozed like sweat.

Though Divine, Jesus' human heart
Of the cross had wanted no part.
But without pain and agony,
Redemption! Healing! Ne'er could be.

When darkness fell, Jesus foreknew
Soldiers would come - not just a few.
Armed for trouble, a fight maybe,
Yet Jesus went SO willingly.

Morning revealed an awful scene.
Could this pulp-mass, human have been?
Scourged and beaten, bruised black and blue.
Was nothing left that man could do?

Little flesh remained, beard half gone,
Look! The pulp-mass moves slowly on
To the hill-top, where all might see,
Jesus was nailed to the cursed Tree.

Three days later, at break of dawn
His life returned with massive yawn.
The price is paid, Redemption won!
Christ reigns on high. Exalted One.

THE FACE OF JESUS

For over a week before writing this poem, I saw a face wherever I went. It had a downward look to the left and I wanted to lift the face up, so I could see the expression clearly. Then two couplets entered my mind and I wrote them down.
'I thought about Jesus the other day and saw the cross in a different way'. 'It was not nails that bound Him to the tree, it was love - for the likes of you and me'.
The poem was obviously about Jesus on the cross. as the poem progressed, the second couplet moved further and further back, until it became the last two lines .

I thought about Jesus the other day
And saw the cross in a different way.
God showed me the face of the Nazarene,
So, I could know how it really had been.

I did not see the crown of thorns He wore,
Nor heard the sound of the crowd's angry roar.
"Release Barrabas, he's the one WE choose.
Away with this man - 'The King of the Jews'."

I saw not the river of blood so red,
Nor yet, what was written above his head.
I saw not the feet that had walked with grace,
For my eyes were riveted on His face.

Two others, they screamed again and again,
I marvelled, for He showed no hint of pain.
Instead, was a look, I could not define,
Then He raised His head and His eyes met mine.

I wanted to run, but knew I MUST stay.
His face told me what He wanted to say.
The look He gave, went through me like a knife,
For now I knew what cost Jesus His life.

It was not for His crimes of deepest dye,
He had never sinned, or spoken one lie.
It was MY sins, that on Jesus were laid,
And the price, was the price I should have paid.

His eyes held mine, I found no words to say.
He'd redeemed ME - there was no other way.
My heart grew warm, I love Him even more.
I'm glad God forgives, does not keep the score.

What his face told me, with you now I share.
You look as well, see what is written there.
It was not nails that bound him to the tree,
It was LOVE - for the likes of you and me.

DESTINY OF FIRE

'Let old Satan lie as much as he will,
Me, I will just point up to Calvary's hill'.
When those words floated into my mind from apparently
nowhere, I was very puzzled and for several weeks, pondered
about what I was supposed to do with them. I repeated the words
over and over to myself, especially the first line. Gradually, it
dawned on me that God wanted me to explain who Satan was
originally; what caused the change, finally how he cleverly
tricks so many people into Hell. See Ezekiel chapter 28: 1 - 19
and Luke chapter 10: 18. This was in the 1990s before I had
a computer, so it took several months to compose, laboriously
recording from one tape recorder to another, time after time,
altering the words and moving the verses around until I was
sure that I had got the facts correct and in the right sequence.
The two lines quoted eventually became the first two of verse
13.

> We were created to be happy and good.
> But, we never can be as good as we should.
> We have an enemy, who stalks us like prey,
> Always seeking to hurt and lead us astray.
>
> Once, he was the finest in God's heavenly land,
> Created to minister at his right hand.
> Lucifer, Son of the morning, was his name.
> He had all that he desired, including fame.
>
> Nothing was denied, to him the angels bowed.
> This went to his head, made him haughty and proud;
> Planned to elevate himself above God's throne,
> But God, who is Lord Supreme, MUST reign alone.

Though God loved him, He had no choice but to say,
"Lucifer sorry, you can no longer stay.
Sin I can not allow, so now you must go.
You and your cronies, get out! Go down below!"

This made him angry, he knew he was to blame.
He swore revenge and vowed to sully God's name.
Since then, many ages have come and have gone.
Millions he's ruined, reeling lies by the ton.

Now called Satan, subtle, so cunning and bright,
He can convince that he's an angel of light.
His evil black self, he is careful to hide
And will NEVER reveal his true darker side

He pretends to be honest, loyal and true.
He promises, "Hey! I'll be a friend to you.
Prosperity, pleasure and fame, all are free.
I have much to offer, put your trust in me.

"You want to go to heaven? That's quite all right.
You stay close to me and I will guide you aright.
Don't trust that man, Jesus, he never was good.
So bad, he was killed on a cross of rough wood."

Foolishly, folk trust him, believe all his lies.
Satan just smiles and hides the gleam in his eyes.
Blindly they follow him, not checking at all,
Do not remember what goes before a fall.

At first, all seems fine as they follow this guide,
The road is crowded, noisy, also is wide.
Soon it is pitch dark and is no longer day.
Folk don't see the road turning a different way.

Now it is winding, steep, slippery as well.
This is but one of many roads down to Hell.
Then folk have arrived, breathed their last and they die,
Know Satan has told them 'one hell of a lie.'

"If only, if only, if ONLY!" they cry.
They cannot come back. There is no second try.
There, with old Satan, for ever they will burn,
And for what might have been, will constantly yearn.

So, let old Satan lie as much as he will.
Me, I will just point up to Calvary's hill
Where Jesus suffered, punished for all OUR sin,
To open Heavens door, that all may go in.

Patiently, God waits, He longs to forgive
When we say, "sorry" and our lives to Him give.
God bears no grudges. Hear His own dear son say,
"For you, I am the Truth, the Life and the Way."

Though we are sinners and deserving to die,
God willingly hears EVERY repentant cry.
He never will say, "I'm too busy today.
Come tomorrow -No! make it another day."

Where are you going? It is vital to know
Our destination while still down here below.
Will YOU accept Jesus and turn to Him now,
Remember His pain and the thorns on his brow?

Then, one day in the future, in Heav'n above,
We will be with Jesus, surrounded by love.
While Satan, who to outshine God did aspire,
With those he tricked will be roasting in the fire.

JESUS IS THE DOOR

I cannot pinpoint how the idea for this one came. It is possible that it was as the result of reading John chapter three, where Nicodemus asked Jesus how to obtain eternal life. I could imagine the situation and wrote it down. The answer Jesus gave and the rest of the poem just flowed from my fingers. Having said that, one line in verse four gave me the biggest problem ever. I quoted something Jesus said and for rhyming purposes, the last word had to be ,sin. Each time I typed His words, it sounded as if I was saying that 'Jesus is sin'. It took ages to sort that one out, but I solved it eventually.

He came by night, "Lord, I appeal to you,
To have Eternal Life, what must I do?"
In John 3, verse 8, the answer is plain.
It is so simple, "You must be Born Again."
Nicodemus frowned, "Please don't joke with me,
I can't go back, Lord, look I am eighty-three."
But Jesus did not mean the human birth,
For that is peculiar to this earth.

"It does not matter to which Faith we hold,
All roads lead to God," is what folk are told,
"Heaven is earned, only by works of man"
Who strive so hard, to do the best they can.
If that is so, tell me, why should it be
Christ died for all, on the Cross of Calvary?
None of us can, for our own sins atone,
Only by blood and God's mercy alone.

John fourteen says, if to God we would come
Only through Jesus, can we reach our home.
Our new Life in Christ will only begin
When forgiven and washed, cleansed from every sin.
The past has then gone, remembered no more.
God cares so much, He will not keep the score.
Take heed to those words, they speak with loud voice,
Like Nicodemus, make Jesus your choice.
He came by night, "Lord, I appeal to you,

If then, to Heaven, your heart does aspire,
Why opt for the other, brimstone and fire?
We all have Free Will, use yours for the right.
Accept God's Pardon and walk in the light.
"Unbelief in Me," Jesus said, "is sin,"
Open your heart and let the Saviour come in.
Those who reject Him - hear these words so true,
To Heaven are barred - don't let that be you!

NEW HOPE

A few years ago, my son spent all night at the hospital, with a friend who tried to take his life, but fortunately failed. God told me to write a poem especially to give him new hope that life is worth living. I included this poem because it could perhaps be the means of preventing yet another near tragedy.

In childhood, life seems all rosy and bright,
Clouds don't exist, only blue, sunny skies.
Homework for exams, take up half the night.
Can't wait to leave school, no regret or sighs.

We then begin work, know we are so smart,
Soon, it's the boss who'll be out of a job.
Slowly we progress, then sadly, we part.
We've changed firms, perhaps married, Gwen or Bob.

"All live happily", so the saying goes.
Life often fails, we rarely find such bliss.
Our plans go wrong, the world seems full of woes.
Can't understand why life goes sour like this.

We feel so lonely, when we've closed the door.
The house is empty, no-one seems to care.
We feel desperate, cry out more and more,
Please come and help me - IF there's Someone there?

Yes, there is, He's the Saviour I have known
Fully trusted, for fifty years or so.
He never has, nor will He let me down,
Since He saved my soul all those years ago.

Don't you know how much the Saviour loves you?
Has no one told you He hears EVERY prayer?
That He LONGS to throw His arms around you
Each tear and heartache really WANTS to share?

He won't turn His back, does not want to know,
When WE ignore Him, want our own sweet way.
Patiently He waits, until WE come to know,
Jesus is The Truth, The Life and The Way.

Will you trust Jesus, all your striving cease,
Remember His pain, the thorns on His brow?
Its such sweet release, just to feel His Peace,
Please let Him come and heal your heart - right now.

THE WAY THERE

The idea for this poem came from something that the Pastor of Elim Church said about eagles flying free up in the high mountains. As usual, I had not the foggiest idea what I was going to write, just sat down and began to write what came into my head, I am often surprised and can hardly believe what appears on the page. This proves that it is not me who composes the poems, but I am the ghost writer for God, though as I said at the beginning, I still have to do the graft of rhyming etc. It was so again in this case. It was not until I responded at the end of verse 1 and God replied at the start of verse 2, that I realised this poem would be a two-way conversation! At least, it was different.

Life is but a journey that takes me home to God.
Many are the valleys, sweet meadows bathed in sun.
Deep rivers I must cross, fierce storms that chill the blood,
Each mountain that I climb, think there, my journey's done.
"I want to stay right here, Lord, on this mountain top,
Everything around is fresh and the air is clean.
Just to see Mount Zion, Lord, makes my heart go 'pop',
But, why is the road there Lord, nowhere to be seen?"

"Because there is no road from there to here my child.
Your route lies along that path, way down there below.
Mountains are but view-points, to spur you on my child,
Now go down, through another valley you must go."

"Not another one, Lord, no birds or flowers fair.
All mine are long, dark and boggy, with sides so high.
Rivers are so hard to cross, when no bridge is there.
Can't I have meadows or mountains where eagles fly?"

"I do see your point child, but your way is not good,
For nothing you will learn, if nothing you endure.
Its valleys and hard trials, rivers thick with mud,
That make you strong and worthy, fit for Heaven's shore."
Since then, I've traversed mountains, valleys, storms as well,
Life is but a journey that takes me home to God.
But, 'Cos I'm not quick to learn, lessons cost me dear,
For, convinced that I knew best, often slipped and fell
'Til repentant, cried; "Lord, what am I doing here?."

Jesus just smiled, "Get up, why stay down there and moan?
Remember, I AM with you, help you climb the stiles.
Keep your eyes on me, child, you'll never walk alone.
Just be happy child, as you trudge those weary miles."
Valleys now are full of light, birds sing songs to me.
Rivers seem but little streams, flowers grace each ford.
I'll even welcome trials, now the truth I see,
That each valley, makes me more like my precious Lord.

A BRAND NEW START

It was the words 'Every day is a new beginning' that started this poem. Where they came from, I do not remember. However, after writing down these words, the rest of the poem, like most of them, appeared to write itself. Many people have told me that this little poem has helped them, for which God has the praise.

Every day, a fresh beginning,
Each morning, a brand new start.
Let go all yesterday's problems,
Don't store them within your heart.

Sorrows retained, just like a stone,
Grow heavier day by day,
Till all your joy and happiness
Take their wings and fly away.

The future then looks, oh so black,
Not a ray of light is seen,
For weeks, or months, you grope around
Remembering what might have been.

Then, in despair, you turn to God,
There, the answer you will find.
Your load WILL lift, as He forgives,
Blows the cobwebs from your mind.

Every day, a fresh beginning,
Each morning, a brand new start.
Thank god for all He's done for you
And Praise Him with ALL your heart.

July 2006

ITS YOUR MOVE

The origin of this poem is almost unbelievable. For years I used a typewriter but could not touch-type because of my hearing problem. When computers came out I went to college and used the 'Word Perfect 5' version for two years until my sight started to go as well. After a year's break, I knew that something had to be done, so rang the college and asked if they could help me. For a while, I had a volunteer who read words to me as they appeared on the screen. This was hilarious, because I constantly asked 'which spelling?' i.e. 'hare or hair?' Fortunately, speech was introduced, So, I was enabled to practice on my own and in this way, at last I learned to touch-type, if only slowly. One day, after enjoying myself typing a full page with whatever came to mind, I scrolled back to check what I had typed. I was astonished when I heard the following words; 'Has no one told you that Jesus loves you?'. Back home I typed those words, then as usual the rest followed naturally, which is this poem. Yet to this day I have no recollection of typing those words.

Has no-one told you that Jesus loves you?
Has no-one told you how deep is his care?
Has no-one told you He died to save you,
That in Heavenly Mansions you might share?

None are perfect while in this human frame.
Sin separates us from the loving God.
All WILL be restored who call on His name,
Forgiven and washed, cleansed in His shed blood.

He paid for your sins, up there on the cross.
Hurting and bleeding, with thorns on his brow.
He willingly came - how great was the cost.
Jesus now pleads, "Please let Me save you NOW."

But, Satan desires to own you as well,
He will stop at NOTHING to gain control.
By lies and deceit, tricks folk into Hell.
The battle is on, the prize is YOUR SOUL.

Time is so short, eternity so long,
No-one knows how little time we have got.
Vital to choose NOW, to whom you belong.
After death - too late, you have tied the knot!

Has no-one told you that Jesus loves you?
Has no-one told you today is the day?
Has no-one told you, it's now up to you?
Accept God's love or, go the other way.

LIVING ON YOUR OWN

During the time I was going blind, I was in the waiting room at the old bus station when I heard two ladies talking about being on their own. Immediately, God told me to write a poem for people who live on their own. At that time, I was not on my own, so had no personal experience to draw on. This poem was just an act of obedience to God's command.

You are on your own, perhaps think it is not fair.
The house is quiet and empty; no-one seems to care;
Once you were a family, now they've all left home,
Scattered here and there and one even lives in Rome.

It's many years since husband Bill died, down at' mine!
Leaving Rachel, Charlotte and David, just turned nine.
You kept busy raising them, had no time for tears,
Guiding and correcting, you also calmed their fears.

Now they've grown and married, leaving you alone.
You find life is not such fun, living on your own.
The house is never dirty, cooking but a chore,
"Is this all the future holds, is there nothing more?"

You and Bill had many friends, now how sad to find
They have their own problems, don't mean to be unkind.
Yet other friends avoid you, look the other way,
Because they feel embarrassed, don't know what to say.

You so long for friendship, but have you ever thought
Of the loving Saviour, who your Salvation bought,
Who died for you on the cross of Calvary.
To forgive your sins, then YOUR friend He wants to be.

Why not take up God's offer, now you're on your own?
With Jesus in your heart, you will never walk alone.
You never need feel lonely, never know despair
Homes are always happy, with Jesus living there.

When your life is over, in Heaven you will be,
Singing our God's praises for all eternity.
Sadly there are some, who in Heaven will not dwell.
They have rejected God, sent themselves to Hell.

NOW IS THE TIME

As usual, do not ask me where this poem came from, because I have no idea. However this time, I decided to write this poem in a light-hearted way for a change. Each verse applies to a different situation; childhood, redundancy, one verse is for ladies, another for the men etc. The refrain at the end of every verse differs slightly. As usual, I had to include the Gospel. Personally, I had a good laugh and enjoyed composing this one.

When your life is bright and rosy,
When you have picked your first posy,
When you have agreed to marry
Your dream man, whose name is Harry.
You see no need to seek the Lord?
It's not too soon to Praise the Lord.

In life you have done oh so well,
Bank balance tinkles like a bell.
Dragged yourself up from out the mire,
Now you have all you can desire.
You don't bother to seek the Lord
Why not give thanks and Praise the Lord.

When you have moved to your dream house,
To your dismay, you see a mouse,
But, your cat's gone out acourting,
When it should be you supporting.
Are you too scared to seek the Lord?
Forget your fear and Praise the Lord?

When you think life has let you down,
Instead of smiles, you get a frown.
Life, it seems, just one big trouble,
Fire has turned your home to rubble.
Here is a chance to seek the Lord.
Now is the time to Praise the Lord.

When all your friends have turned their back,
And then, the Boss gives you the sack.
What to do when the money's spent?
Sink your pride and live in a tent.
Remind yourself to seek the Lord.
Have a good laugh and Praise the Lord.

When you have crashed your wife's new car,
Will your excuses stretch that far?
When you've messed up that simple job,
She leaves you for your best friend, Bob.
How about now to seek the Lord?
So, come on lads and Praise the Lord.

God offers us free Salvation,
He makes just one stipulation,
We MUST choose our destination.
This applies to EVERY nation.
All entitled to seek the Lord,
Why not join in and Praise the Lord?

We make our choice from only two.
Heaven or Hell, its up to you.
God wants us all with Him to dwell.
Satan prefers we 'go to Hell'.
Be serious now to seek the Lord,
So start right away to Praise the Lord!

I've decided, I made my choice,
That's why I sing, why I rejoice.
Its your turn now, you too must choose,
Will you accept, will you refuse?
Don't hesitate to seek the Lord,
Make up your mind to Praise the Lord.

If you should pass the Saviour by,
When the time comes for you to die
You decided, you've chosen hell.
So, for ever, you there must dwell.
Far too late then to seek the Lord,
How you will wish you'd praised the Lord.

If you chose right, then when you die,
Michael's boat will come sailing by
To row you to that other shore,
To live with God for evermore.
How glad you'll be you sought the Lord,
Eternally, to Praise the Lord.

SONGS OF DAVID

This poem happened while I was thinking about David and all he went through in his life both before and after he became King of Israel.

I often think of David
And the trials he went through.
His was not an easy path,
But knew what his God could do.

He learned this while still a boy,
Caring for his father's sheep.
Through lessons hard, learned to trust.
Knew that God his soul would keep.

This showed through in his own life,
Guarding well flocks in his care.
Was expert with stone and sling,
Killing both lion and bear.

He praised God with special songs,
Wrote them down with pen so sharp.
Lambs sat quiet while he sang,
Playing music on his harp.

God chose David to be King.
Over all Israel he reigned.
But, he kept a humble heart,
Never thought he 'had it made'.

I love to think of David
And how well he battled through.
I'll sing the Songs of David,
For his God is my God too.

From me too, God wants to drive
The things that I should not do.
Till I learn, as David learned,
What is pleasing, Lord, to you.

The past I'll leave behind me,
Give to God my pain and woe.
Try to emulate David
Daily, more like Christ to grow.

Then, one day, in Heaven we'll meet,
Talk of all our God has done.
Give the Glory all to him,
And Jesus, His own dear Son.

2007

The next five poems were written in the late 1980's while I was sitting in the summer house where I was then living.

NOAH'S ARK

This speaks for itself. It can be sung to a well-known children's play song. On one occasion it was sung and enjoyed by members of Calvary Church, Macclesfield.

The people thought it just a lark,
When Noah built himself an Ark.
For God had said, rain soon would pour,
Something they had not seen before.

No one believed old Noah,
No one believed old Noah,
No one believed old Noah,
So, only eight were saved.

The animals went in two by two,
Elephant, Bear and Kangaroo.
Then the Noahs, their sons and wives,
God had promised to save their lives.

The sky grew dark and gloomy,
The sky grew dark and gloomy,
The sky grew dark and gloomy,
And only eight were saved.

The rain it soon came pelting down,
The folk then knew they all would drown.
So they began to rant and roar,
But, God had firmly closed the door.

Now they all believed it,
Now they all believed it,
Now they all believed it,
But, only eight were saved.

The rain came down, the Ark went up,
Water covered each mountain top.
Through the window, all Noah could see,
Was lots of nothing - just the sea.

The rain it fell in torrents,
The rain it fell in torrents,
The rain it fell in torrents,
Still only eight were saved.

Forty days then the rain it stopped,
Out of the Ark, animals hopped,
Into a world they did not know,
Soon far and wide, they all did go.

The Noahs had more children,
The Noahs had more children,
The Noahs had more children,
And filled the land again.

Though God had said, it still would rain,
He never would flood the world again.
To keep His promise, He would show,
On each bright cloud, a huge rainbow.

So, now you know the story,
Let us give God the Glory,
So, now you know the story
Why only eight were saved.

December 2006

SOLITUDE

Again, this poem speaks for itself, because the reason it was written is in the poem, so there is no need to repeat it here.

I have no one to pray with me,
Oh, how often I do declare.
No one seems to understand,
No one appears to even care.

I go to Church, sing the hymns,
What Pastor says, I try to do.
Read my Bible, but when I pray,
Do not seem able to get through.

I love Jesus, I really do
And I long to serve Him better,
But, even though I pray alone,
My God knows I am no quitter!

God says He will always answer
If only two or three will pray.
So, how can I expect answers
When I pray on my own each day?

Some folk have friends to call their own.
They do not have to pray alone
But me, tell me, who have I got,
I have no one, I pray alone.

Please Lord, may I have someone too,
A prayer partner with whom to be.
Then together, we'll pray to you,
More productive, don't you agree?

One prayer night, someone spoke in Tongues,
Then, the Interpretation came,
"Alone, but not alone my child,"
It was as if God spoke my name.

I mused for days on those few words
I pondered long, was still not sure.
I am alone, but not alone,
Why did they have to be obscure?.

"Oh please, my Lord," I prayed that night,
god knows I don't intend to moan.
"Will you explain this truth to me,
I am alone, but not alone?"

He told me in a still small voice,
This hushed my heart, His words were clear.
"My Son, Spirit and you, make three,
So, you three pray and I will hear."

Jesus, Spirit and me, all pray?
I tried this out, the time just flew.
Now we three pray, others do too.
God hears us all, praise Him, that's true.

I'm glad that precious truth sank in,
To heaven, I lift up my hand,
I pray alone, but not alone,
Thanks Lord; at last I understand.

April 2008

GREATER WORKS

This poem developed from the verse in the Bible where Jesus told his disciples they could do greater things. " I tell you the truth, anyone who has faith in me will do what I have been doing. He will do even greater things than these because I am going to the Father." John 14 : 12

I read this truth in God's Good Book:
From nothing He made everything.
How Jesus died and rose again,
He will return and reign as King.

When Jesus walked upon this earth
Many miracles He performed.
The blind could see, the lame could walk,
God loves you all, folk were informed.

Jesus sent His Disciples out
To all the countryside around,
To do the same as he had done.
To heal the sick and loose the bound.

They all returned, so jubilant,
They'd done all he had done - and more!
"Rather rejoice," they then were warned,
"To win a soul for Heaven's shore."

When Jesus walked upon the sea,
Peter tried it, but came off worst.
He too, was startled, somewhat awed,
When Jesus, that old fig tree cursed.

Jesus said, Oh, that was nothing
To what with faith, they all would see,
For they could tell a large mountain,
"Get up, throw yourself in the sea."

In life, we have many mountains,
Naturally, not that rocky kind.
He meant the many obstacles,
That we, in His dear Name, must bind.

The Bible says, that Greater Works
Than He did, we can also do.
Why then, as we have permission,
We fail and do not make it so?

Sin and sickness are all around,
How much we long to see them gone.
Let us be bold in Jesus' name
As James and Peter said, and John.

Silver and gold we may not have,
But something worth oh, so much more.
It is our faith that we must share,
Pray for the sick and feed the poor.

Remember, it is our faith, plus God
Will bring about those Greater Works,
But, when we want our own sweet way
Find, THAT is where the danger lurks.

So, as we start each new fresh week,
Forget whatever was before.
Begin again, those Greater Works,
God with us, that's the Winning Score.

February 2007

WHY WORRY?

This was originally written for a member of my family who was a real worrier. However, recently I decided to rewrite it, so it would apply to a much wider need.

Once you were a sinner, knew nought of God's great Love.
You lived your own life, a life where God had no part.
Then you met the Saviour, who came from heaven above
To forgive your sins, then to Him, you gave your heart.

Your love for God shines through, as everyone can tell.
You've changed dramatically from what you were before.
Yet, you seem distracted, your mind on past things dwell.
Are you still worrying, or is there something more?

Why do you still worry? God knows you inside out.
He knows your every need: employment, food and home.
Your side is to fully trust, don't give place to doubt.
Your life is safe with Him, wherever you may roam.

Jesus said "Don't worry," He means just that you know.
Have you not discovered there's nought he cannot do?
Only the good things, on you he will bestow.
Don't hesitate to ask, believe it will be so.

Check Matthew 6 verse 19, read on to the end.
How God cares for animals, birds and flowers too.
They neither work nor reap solely on him depend.
Yet, you still cling to worry, this really will not do.

You would not lie or steal; you know that to be wrong
But, worry is a sin, in essence just as bad,
Because it always weakens, NEVER makes you strong.
It results in sadness, but faith will make you glad.

When you feel forsaken, while walking on life's road.
Do you ask God for help, perhaps unsure He knows?
Think that all on your own, you must carry your load,
Solving your problems, tossed by every wind that blows.

God, He will not ask you, for you to live your life
On your own, unaided, with no one there to care.
He knows you'll often fail and fall down in the strife.
He says, "Come unto Me, let Me your burdens bear."

Jesus said, "Without Him, there is nothing we can do."
Grapes only take their life, when joined to the vine.
You are joined to Jesus, you to Him, Him to you.
Giving life to others, filled with His Love Divine.

Why then, do you worry? It only does you harm.
You're the one who suffers, if "Worry rules, OK."
I can think of nothing worse. To dispel your calm.
Evict that worry; refuse to let it stay.

March 14th 2007

A CONCISE JOB

This poem is the book of Job 'in a nutshell' in a manner of speaking. A few years ago, I re-wrote and amplified it, as far as possible, using actual quotes from the KJ translation. I hope this intrigues people to read the whole of this fantastic book for themselves.
Many years ago, I gave a Minister a copy of the original version and still have his letter of appreciation, but think he would prefer this new one if he is still around.

God held Court one day, up there in the Heavenly Realm,
All of his Angels and old Satan too, had come.
"What have you been up to Satan, where did you roam?"
"Wandering round the world, observing all You've done."
"Did you see my servant Job? None so good as he.
Notice how he loves me, as faithful as can be?"

"Sure, I saw the thorn hedge you have placed around him,
Made it strong and safe, secure from all my wiles.
No wonder he's perfect, no wonder he smiles,
How different it would be, if nothing went his way,
Just let me get at him, open a little space,
I'll take all he has, THEN he'll curse you to Your face."

Now God was confident and God, He was serene,
Trust in His servant Job was both solid and sure.
"OK, you try him, but I know he will stay pure.
Take from him what you like, all is in your power.
Just one thing you cannot do, one thing I will not stand,
You must not touch Job's life, I trust you understand."

That day was black for Job, murdered were his children.
All his sheep and camels, his servants too, were dead.
Boils, they were just EVERYWHERE, even on his head.
Poor Job was desolate, what was he to do?
He'd lost all, except his wife -could not feel much worse,
He then cursed everything, but, God he would not curse.

Three Comforters arrived, shocked at what they saw.
Seven days and nights they sat, not a sound was heard.
Job's suffering and pain, was far too deep for words.
Eventually, he spoke, God's confidence was proved.
"God gives so liberally, He also takes away.
I owe all to Him. So, His must be the last say."

Then in turn, each one spoke, what they implied was clear.
Job must have greatly sinned, for God to treat him so.
Job was implacable, refused to let Truth go.
Asked, "Can a man be just before Almighty God?
When I die, in my flesh, know, God on earth I'll see
But, can man stand before Him, in sincerity?"

A fourth man was listening, Elihu was his name.
"My words shall reflect the uprightness of my heart.
Job says he's righteous, but only speaks truth in part.
Utters words without knowledge, words without wisdom,
Says, "I've no transgressions, am innocent and clean.
God counts me enemy, my feet in stocks are seen."

41

"Job, stop and consider the wondrous works of God.
He orders clouds to form, commands wind, hail and frost.
Directs where rain shall fall, so not a drop is lost."
Then, out of the whirlwind, God's voice like thunder, spoke.
Reminded Job, from nothing He's made all things good.
Moonbeams dancing on the sea, darting where they would.

He asked, "Are you greater than Me, Almighty God?
Can you make trees and plants, then can you make them grow,
Sun, moon and twinkling stars, treasures of the snow,
Who hung the world in space? For nothing came by chance.
Who rotates the seasons, limits the raging sea?
Gird your loins, be a man, for now you must answer Me?"

Job knew he'd been arrogant, asked God to forgive.
His three friends God reproved, said, Job for them MUST pray.
This he did, God forgave and sent them on their way.
Job had more children, servants, sheep and camels too.
For God had made this promise, to Job He would restore,
Twice as much of everything, than he had before.

February 2007

A LIFE OF BLISS

Sadly, one does hear from time to time of marriages going wrong, even among Christians. In 1997, I felt constrained to write this poem to help newly-weds to make a success or others to improve their marriage. Why God asked me to do this, I do not know. Over the years since, I have given framed copies of this poem to several newly-weds and hope it has helped them. An article entitled 'Life is a Garden' has developed from this poem.

You have taken your Vows, so now are Man and Wife,
Think not a single thing can mar YOUR married life,
But problems they will come, as problems always do,
I will help you to avoid them, with a hint or two.

First, think of your future as a very large field,
The seed that you plant there is the crop it will yield.
Think very carefully of the crop that you grow,
Remember the maxim, "You reap just what you sow."

Plant twelve rows of Kisses, plant twenty rows of Love,
Plant Time for each other and Time for God above.
Plant ten rows of Give and Take, these are Love's Commands,
Don't forget the bushes of Hugs and Holding Hands.

Don't plant Bitterness, Anger, Arguments or Strife,
Or you will lose the joy you should have with your wife.
Here is another saying, "Look before you leap,"
Then, do not plants the crops you have no wish to reap.

The Field of Life is yours, to do with as you will.
Make it a field of joy, not just a bitter pill.
Remember, say "I love you", every single day,
So, I will leave you now, to ponder what I say.

March 2007

MY PRAYER

This poem is a prayer of repentance to God when we make a hash of things as we often do, but want to declare that we love Him and with His help still want to be with him in Heaven.

"I'm sorry Lord, I'm in this mess,
Cleanse me from all unrighteousness.
From sin and doubt, my pathway block,
Secure me, Lord, to Christ, the Rock.

So now upon this Rock I'll lean,
Until Your wonderous face I've seen.
I've caught a glimpse of yonder light,
City of gold and harbour bright.

I know the road there will be rough,
But, if You're with me, that's enough.
Though there'll be times when I fall down,
You'll never leave me, there to drown.

Lord, I cannot do this alone,
I need Your help to guide me home.
So, for this Grace I do implore,
To reach my Goal, on Heaven's shore.

When in that happy throng I stand,
Then at last, I will understand.
Greet my friends and family too,
But, best of all, I'll be with You."

March 2008

BLIND MEMORIES

This is a poem that is based on my memories of a town that I know well and the changes there, that I cannot see, so choose to remember this town as I knew it.
When I remarked to someone, that this poem would be of no interest to someone in a different town, I was told I was mistaken. They would relate my memories to their memories of their town and their reaction to changes there would be the same as mine.

PART ONE - THEN

Once I could see to the far horizon,
Start of the day and the red sinking sun.
Trawlers left the harbour, at cool grey dawn
Hardly before the new day had been born.

They sailed far away to the Northern Sea,
For many long hours no land they would see.
They trawled to catch fish, with both might and main,
Ere turning for home and loved ones again.

On Whitehaven's South Shore, content to bide,
Watched for their return, on the late high tide.
The cannon reminded, of John Paul Jones,
How he spiked the guns - and of dead men's bones.

Then, to the horizon, I strained to see
The first wee black speck, where sky meets the sea.
First I saw one, then two, then there were three.
Soon there were dozens, so it seemed to me.

The specks grew larger, till boats they became,
They all passed so close I could read each name.
Then they were gone, round Whitehaven's south Shore,
To unload their catch, then trawl out for more.

A sea-front scrap yard, I know you agree,
Was hardly the thing to see from the sea.
Pleasure craft crazily leaned to one side,
When they are abandoned by ebbing tide.

A rummage shop once was on Roper Street,
Clothes littered the floor, not hung up so neat.
Rail lines then ran, 'twixt station and Haig Pit,
Coals to Newcastle? not a bit of it.

Many were the mines in Whitehaven then.
Cutting the coal employed most of the men.
They toiled with bent backs, hands blistered and sore,
In tunnels that stretched for three miles or more.

That work was hard, but what else could they do?
They had not the options, open to you.
Heartbreak and death were but their way of life,
No woman knew how long she'd be a wife.

Young children as well were sent down the mines,
Instead of learning three times three makes nine.
Folk had to live-there was no other way,
But, when mines blew up, why should children pay?

In St Nic's Churchyard, engraved on each side
Of a large white stone, names of children who died.
The stone is still there, near the Duke Street gate,
All too young to die, some were not yet eight.

PART TWO - CHANGES

Thank God, those hard times are over and gone,
Let us pause to remember, then move on.
Trawlers don't catch fish, nor men toil below,
So, where in this town for work, do men go?

They say, 'Tempus fugit' time will march on,
It stopped in one place, there still is Marchon.
Goods for Marchon once came in ships so large,
Then were transferred to a much smaller barge.

At Workington now, unloading is done,
giving van drivers a seven-mile run.
Sellafield is only miles down the road,
They still need more folk, to share their workload.

Tesco now is, where an hotel once stood
Serving the townsfolk, as really it should.
The scrapyard now is a beautiful place
To sit in comfort, the sun on your face.

Pleasure craft now no embarrassment feel,
For no ebbing tide exposes their keel.
They have a Marina right up to date,
They really love it, sit proudly in state.

All Whitehaven's seafront has been re-vamped.
With a brand new image it has been stamped.
A Resort it is hoped it will become
And folk be tempted to make here, their home.

PART THREE - NOW

Sadly, I have now lost most of my sight,
Sometimes I wonder is it day or night.
I get frustrated, so often at home,
Wish I was still free, on my own to roam.

To read, knit and paint are out, so must find
Other occupations to fill my mind.
To learn fresh skills, gives me something to do,
Computer and dancing, to name but two.

I can go shopping, if taken of course,
But, don't have much chance at the shops to pause.
There's so little time, so much work to do,
It seems I am back 'ere the door I'm through.

At Whitehaven it's different, time to spare,
There is time to look, to stop and to stare
At all the changes I'm told are now there,
So, I no longer know where what is where.

Down at the harbour most changes are found,
To me this is now unfamiliar ground.
I'll not condemn changes, maybe they're good,
To me, they're about as clear as thick mud.

Because these changes mean nothing to me,
I choose to see them as they used to be.
Once, to where I headed I walked straight there,
How I wish I still knew where what is where?

No longer abandoned by ebbing tide,
Yet I still see 'Freya', lean to one side.
I still avoid rail lines I know were there,
Taking the coal, well, to goodness knows where.

Yes, I still go to Whitehaven's South Shore,
Pretend that the boats are trawling once more.
The fish-wharf jetty is now a short pier,
Memories flood back, to the folk who worked here.

The lighthouse has not got right up and gone,
It still beams out light when each day is done.
The candlestick-shaped chimney, is still there,
How I wish I still knew, where what is where.

From Bransty, recall a wonderful view,
Isle of Man, Scotland and North Ireland too.
On very clear days, this may make you smile,
I KNOW I have seen the Emerald Isle.

Marrow to me, is the kind that I eat,
'Marra', to men here, is the friend they greet.
An unopened flower is called a 'bud',
Here, in Whitehaven, a bird is a 'bud'.

I must make mention of Whitehaven folk,
Happy they're now freed from the mines' hard yoke.
They are resilient, strong and so brave,
Willingly to me their friendship they gave.

This is the end of my memory-lane walk,
Hope you have enjoyed my chatter and talk.
The fishermen and boats, scrapyard and mines,
Are snapshots of memory, etched on my mind.
June 2007

LIFE IS A GARDEN

The Bible clearly states that the man is the steward of his marriage and it is he and he alone, who will give account to God for its success - or otherwise.

I am glad to say that we women also have a part to play by supporting our husbands and helping to maintain a happy and stable environment for the family which is also a VERY important role, if you stop to think about it.

For some reason I feel that God wants me to write this article for newly married men and perhaps as a reminder, a gentle one, to more mature men, just how vital and important their role as head of the house, husband and father really is in the sight of God, and how, together, husband and wife can make or improve their married bliss.

Now do not worry. I have decided to write this article in an amusing and light-hearted way. Then, hopefully, no one will get the impression that I will be dictatorial or that they are being preached at and so take offence, because none is intended.

Gardening is a hobby or job that many men can relate to. So, in the following descriptions of four very different types of fictitious men, I will refer to them as "Head Gardeners" and will deliberately draw them somewhat larger than life, because it is a well-known fact that exaggeration often makes a point more easily remembered. Well, that is the theory anyway! Now let us see if it works in practice.

Bob - Head Gardener 1

Bob had been very interested in gardening ever since his Dad had taken him to his allotment when he was around five years old. When Bob left school, he enrolled for a gardening course at the local college, which he passed with honours He began work at The Manor, in his local town, where he soon rose to Head Gardener. As the result, when Bob moved into 1, Acacia Avenue, the first house to be built on a new development, the sight of all the tin cans, lumps of cement and other rubbish that the builders were too lazy to take with them, was more an annoyance than a problem. He then tested the soil to see whether it was acid or alkaline. He browsed through a catalogue he had picked up at the local Garden Centre. Naturally, he knew what he wanted. Then he spotted a picture of three new varieties of a certain bush that would be well suited to the type of soil in his garden. Even the names appealed to him. They were Love, Joy and Happiness. Each flowered at different times of the Spring and Summer. Not only that, each had its own distinctive colour and fragrance. They were expensive, but would look good at the front of the house and give pleasure to others as well as himself. He bought one bush of each variety, choosing the ones with the strongest and most vigorous growth.

They were planted and watered as soon as he arrived home, because he had already thoroughly dug the ground over, putting in manure and other essential nutrients that would help them to adapt to their new environment.

They were given extra water in dry spells and protected against predators and whenever frost threatened during the winter. All that care and attention to detail naturally paid off. When his beautiful bushes of Love, Joy and Happiness came into full bloom, everyone around came to admire them and enjoy their heady fragrance and more often than not, was given cuttings and advice on how to achieve the same dazzling success.

Alan -Head Gardener 2

Alan was always full of good intentions and high hopes. When he enrolled for a gardening course at his local college, he had intended to emerge with the highest possible qualifications, but sadly, most of what he was supposed to learn, went straight through, because his mind was perpetually somewhere else.

The summer after Bob moved into Acacia Avenue and his bushes of Love, Joy and Happiness were opening into full bloom, Alan also moved into the same avenue. Alan was really impressed and wanted to have a garden to equal that of his neighbour. So, the next Spring, he asked Bob where he could buy some. Bob gave Alan all the advice he could. However, when Alan arrived at the Garden centre he was faced with hundreds of bushes of every description, shape and size. What was worse, they all looked similar at that stage of development. Also, being certain that he would recognise them he did not buy a catalogue, which would not have helped, for he had forgotten to ask the names of the bushes.

He bought the ones that looked like the right ones and took them home in triumph. Suddenly, it began to rain quite heavily, which made it a 'no go' job as far as clearing away all the tin cans, lumps of cement and other rubbish the builders had left behind and planting was concerned. He fully intended to do it the next evening after work. However, it had not stopped raining and the ground looked boggy. Then Alan had what he thought was a brilliant idea. He donned a rain mac, dashed out, pushed the rubbish to one side in three places and plonked the bushes in, then retreated back inside the house.

Several weeks later, the bushes looked far from happy, but surprisingly, they survived that early ordeal. Alan was in for a shock the next year when Bob's bushes of Love, Joy and happiness came into flower and Alan's were not even in bud. They were not even remotely like Bob's; they had no fragrance and were ugly in comparison. Poor Alan, his good intentions lay in ruins and his high hopes dashed to smithereens. He shook his head sadly, he had really intended to have a beautiful garden.

You see, at the college, everything he heard had gone in one ear and straight out through the other. Consequently, his 'intention of becoming a highly qualified Head Gardener had not *exactly* come to fruition. Surprisingly, the bushes did survive that early ordeal, in spite of Alan.

The next year when Bob's bushes of Love, Joy and Happiness came into flower, Alan's bushes were not even in bud. Nor were they even remotely like Bob's. They had no fragrance and were ugly in comparison.

Poor Alan. His good intentions lay in ruins and his high hopes dashed to smithereens. He shook his head sadly; he had really intended to have a beautiful garden.

Fortunately, Bob was able to persuade him that all was not lost and dig the wrong bushes out and replace them with the right ones the next year. Then how glad he was that he had listened to Bob's good advice.

Jeremy - Head Gardener 3

Jeremy was one of the nicest guys you could wish to meet, but his problem was that he suffered from very muddled-up thinking. So if he got anything right, it was a miracle. When he moved into Acacia Avenue, he was yet another admirer of Bob's bushes of Love, Joy and Happiness and yes, he wanted some too. Bob told him the way to the Garden Centre; gave him the names and offered to lend him his own catalogue, but as usual everything got mixed up in Jeremy's brain, so it was fortunate that the Garden Centre was not far away, otherwise, muddled-up Jeremy would never have found it. There he was faced with what seemed to be acres and acres of plants, bushes and trees of every shape and size. At the enquiry desk, the assistant could not grasp what Jeremy wanted, because his description was muddled up; nor could he remember the names of the bushes. Understandably, it was either chance or a miracle that Jeremy bought the right bushes of Love, Joy and Happiness.

At home, he planted his acquisition in the garden; well, somewhere in the garden, that is. Jeremy just dug a hole and dropped the young bushes in, wherever he fancied among the now rusty tin cans, lumps of cement and the other rubbish that the builders had not bothered to take with them. 'So what!' None of that would be seen once the bushes had grown, was his reasoning.

When Jeremy saw how much time Bob spent watering and tending everything that was now in his garden, he thought that was a complete waste of time. He reasoned that as nature provided both sun and rain, why not leave it to nature's discretion? So he let his bushes and nature make their own arrangements.

When Bob's bushes of Love, Joy and happiness bloomed and the fragrance wafted over into Jeremy's garden, he knew it was high time to inhale the heady fragrance and admire his own dazzling display of Love, Joy and Happiness.

Jeremy went into the garden, but where was his dazzling display of Love, Joy and Happiness? He looked all round, but he could not remember where in the garden he had planted them. Not that it would have mattered, because by then thistles, briars and other weeds had taken over and were making a dazzling display of their own. His bushes of Love, Joy and Happiness had been denied access to essential air, sunshine and water, so had given up the ghost and died of malnutrition.

To say that Jeremy was devastated was the understatement of *that* year. He just stood there uncomprehendingly. As we have seen, dear thinking was not exactly Jeremy's forte, so as he saw no way round this, he moved to a tiny flat where there was no garden to remind him of what might have been.

Rupert - Head Gardener 4

White Rupert was having a driving lesson, he and his instructor happened to pass the Acacia development that was nearing completion. It was the first time that Rupert had been outside the Inner City tenement, in a very large city where he had grown up.

It was so different that he could not keep his mind on his driving, so the instructor let him stop the car. Then they walked around to admire the houses and pretty gardens. He could not believe that such places existed.

After successfully passing the test a few weeks later, he bought a small car and drove to have a more detailed look at Acacia Avenue. To his delight, the very last house to be built on Acacia Avenue was for sale. He bought it and moved in days after the last of Bob's bushes of Love, Joy and Happiness came into full blossom. Rupert's amazement knew no bounds and he thought they were the most beautiful flowers he had ever seen. Of course they were. They were the only ones he had ever seen!

Consequently, he assumed that everything grew naturally. So he planted nothing. He waited and waited all that year and the one after that, to see in his garden, green lawns, border plants and bushes of Love, Joy and Happiness appear in his garden, as they did in those of his neighbours. He waited for a few more years, but his garden remained in the same state of dereliction as when he had moved in. Well, except for a gorgeous display of thistles, briars etc., that nature had kindly provided to cover up the ugliness of the now rusty tin-cans, lumps of cement and all the other rubbish the builders had neglected to remove. Rupert thought it was very unfair of his garden to provide dazzling displays of Love Joy and Happiness for his neighbours and none for himself. When Bob had offered to help Rupert, he had brushed the offer off, rather brusquely, so was left to his own devices. He turned against his garden and from then on, threw every bit of his rubbish all over it in retaliation. Eventually, his mind went and he spent the rest of his life in a mental institution.

In the above illustrations, I described Love, Joy and Happiness as being bushes for convenience. Now I will refer to them as 'seeds', which in the context of this article is more accurate. From the day a man marries, he plants seeds of some kind into his marriage, although he is not aware of it. You see, like seeds planted in the garden, these seeds also reproduce their own kind and are either positive or negative. You will see what I mean as we progress.

I will now briefly recap each fictitious Head Gardener and how he reacted to his garden. Then, alongside it I will describe a fictitious husband of similar nature and his reaction to his marriage, which will show how closely they parallel each other.

Human nature being what it is, it is doubtful if a real life husband will be an exact replica of the illustration, but more likely a combination of one or more. As I said at the beginning, my aim is not to criticise, but only to highlight possible problem areas so they can be dealt with if need be. So off we go again.

Bob - Head Gardener 1

Bob was a sensible young man. To achieve his ambition, he knew this meant much study. When years later, he moved into Acacia Avenue, he did all the right things so that the bushes of Love, Joy and Happiness, plus everything else he planted had every chance of being successful. He was then in a position to help others to achieve the same dazzling results as well. At the end of his life, Bob was satisfied, knowing that he had helped at least some of his neighbours.

Terry - Fictitious Husband 1

Terry was also sensible. Before embarking on marriage, he too, prepared the ground, as it were. He followed the example set by his own parents. He carefully considered every aspect that he could think of and asked himself many question such as: Was he capable, as well as willing to take on the responsibility of providing for a wife and hopefully children on a lifelong basis? Was he prepared to admit that he would make mistakes? If he did, would he run away at the first frown, or talk it over with his wife until together, they found either a solution, or at least, an acceptable compromise?

Only when he was satisfied with his answers, did he propose to the girl he loved. Consequently, Terry only planted in his marriage the positive seeds that would produce the results he wanted to reap from it, which were, Love, Joy and Happiness. He nurtured those precious seeds with the same consideration that Bob nurtured his bushes. He did this by giving her lots of hugs and kisses; taking interest in what she wore; what she was doing; when she was tired, he insisted that she rested for a while and *never* forgot to tell her on a daily basis, just how much he loved her. Naturally, all this care and attention ensured that his marriage was equally successful as the bushes in Bob's garden. When his neighbours asked him what the secret was for his dazzlingly happy marriage, he always quoted this maxim: "Only sow what you want to reap and do not plant what you have no wish to reap.'

Alan - Head Gardener 2

Alan with his head in the clouds and his feet dangling somewhere between there and the ground.

If an A-level could be achieved by Good Intentions and High Hopes, he would have passed with honours.

He went to the Garden Centre with every intention of buying what he hoped were bushes of Love, Joy and happiness like Bob's, which he took home. Then it started to rain non-stop for several days. Alan had no intention of getting soaked so he plonked them in anywhere and by the time the sun came out the bushes looked very sorry for themselves. He intended to nurture them like he saw Bob do, but good intentions were all that Alan possessed.

It was only when Bob's bushes flowered and gave off heady perfume and his bore no pretty flowers and were ugly in comparison, that Alan realised he had planted the wrong ones, which was glaringly obvious for all to see. That is how Alan learned the hard way that the path of Good Intentions leads precisely - nowhere! It is to his credit that the following year Alan listened to Bob's advice, rooted out the wrong bushes and replaced them with the right ones. Then he too, achieved what he really wanted, which was a dazzling display of Love, Joy and Happiness of his own.

Simon - Fictitious Husband 2

Like Alan, Simon could have gained an A-level in Good Intentions and High Hopes.

He had not even been listening when, two years before, his Dad had given him the usual Father/Son good advice on how to achieve a happy and successful marriage, because he was full of the over-confidence of youth. Consequently, he got himself into a mess with the first pretty girl who smiled at him and rushed into an early marriage, without doing any pre-marriage homework, hoping it would work out.

On the eve of their wedding, Simon promised his equally young bride there would be no clouds in *their* sky and everything would be Love, Joy and Happiness. Sadly, after a year or two, there was no sign of the Love, Joy and Happiness that every man craves, because he had planted negative seeds of irritability, bad temper, lack of consideration for her welfare, or when she was tired; did not notice when she dressed up to please him; complained when his meal was five minutes late; was angry when she told him how lonely it was every evening when the children were in bed and he was on the golf course or in the Clubhouse with his mate, instead of the positives ones of making her feel important to him; showing her love in the general sense; keeping her well supplied with hugs and kisses; assurances every single day that he loved her.

Matters came to a head when she threatened to leave him for someone else who did love her and made her feel wanted and appreciated. That was how Simon learned the hard way where the path of good intentions leads. Over the years, Simon had noticed how dazzlingly happy his neighbours, Terry and his wife were, so listened when Terry explained where he had gone wrong, then helped Simon root out the negative habits and replace them with the Love, Joy and Happiness that he longed for. Simon's wife liked the difference in her husband and together they changed their rocky marriage for a dazzlingly happy one, like that of Terry and his wife.

Jeremy - Head Gardener 3

As we saw, Jeremy was adept at creating chaos out of order, if you know what I mean, so, it was either chance or a miracle that he managed to buy the right bushes of Love, Joy and Happiness. After planting them, he left their future in nature's care, unaware that nature required *some* help from him.

When Bob's bushes of Love, Joy and Happiness and heady fragrance caused their usual stir, Jeremy remembered his, but because he had little care for the welfare of his bushes, he could not find them. Thistles, briars and other weeds had covered up the ugliness of what the builders had neglected to take with them. So they had been either choked or died of malnutrition. Jeremy's muddled-up mind could see no way round this disaster so he lost interest in the garden and went to live in a tiny flat where there was no garden to remind him of the Love, Joy and Happiness that could have been his.

Stuart - Fictitious Husband 3

Stuart's muddled-up mind ensured that he was in hot water more often than out of it. It was a relief to his parents when, in his late thirties he got married. His parents had set an excellent example of married bliss, but that had not sunk in Stuart's brain, so how he managed to plant *some* positive seeds of Love, Joy and Happiness into his wife's heart will forever remain a mystery.

For a while, all did appear to be well. Then, satisfied that he had 'made it' as a good husband, Stuart became complacent and sat back on his laurels, because like Jeremy, he thought that once Love, Joy and Happiness had been planted, they would continue to grow and flourish without the need of further demonstrations from himself. Consequently, when only a few years later, his wife told him that it was obvious he did not love her and wanted a divorce to marry a man who cared deeply for her Stuart could have been knocked down with a feather.

Clear thinking was not exactly Stuart's forte either. He could not accept that it was his neglect of the needs of the wife he truly loved that had caused this. When the divorce was finalised, he moved to another part of the country where there was nothing to remind him of what might have been.

Rupert - Head Gardener 4

When Rupert moved into Acacia Avenue, he was very impressed with Bob's dazzling display of Love, Joy and Happiness bushes and understandably wanted to see them growing in his own garden. The problem was that Rupert grew up in a noisy environment in a large city where milk came in plastic bottles and everything else was bought in supermarkets. He had no idea that potatoes, vegetables, trees, plants, flowers etc, do not grow naturally but had to be planted. Consequently he planted nothing in his garden; he just waited for the bushes of Love, Joy and Happiness to appear, as they obviously did in his neighbours' gardens, but no bushes of Love, Joy and Happiness showed up even after waiting for several years. On the other hand, thistles, weeds and briars made a colourful substitute, to the annoyance of his neighbours. Rupert could not understand why his garden had not given him Love, Joy and Happiness and his neighbours had them in abundance. So blamed the garden for not co-operating with him. He turned against it and returned to the city of his youth. However he could not settle. His mind went and he died in a mental institution.

Oliver - Fictitious Husband 4

When both his parents were killed tragically, there were no relatives to care for the three years old Oliver, so he spent his childhood years in an orphanage, where at fourteen, he was tipped out to fend for himself on the streets. As a result, he fell in with the wrong company and got himself into the kind of trouble that earned him a prison sentence. On his release, he was provided with a room in a hostel and offered a job in a cotton mill, where he met and dated a girl who, like himself, was also on her own.

It was not long before they drifted into marriage. His years at the Orphanage in that era had been more an existence than a preparation for life. Consequently, Oliver was unaware that it was his job to plant in his marriage, what he wanted to reap from it. He planted no positive seeds of love, consideration, reminders that he loved his pretty wife. Yet he longed to see the Love, Joy and happiness that other couples seemed to enjoy. Although Oliver did not deliberately sow negative seeds of irritability, neglect of her needs and so on, the effect on his marriage was exactly the same. Oliver waited and waited in vain. When year succeeded year and Love, Joy and Happiness failed to blossom, he grew more and more morose, for it did not even enter his head that the main fault lay with himself. The result was that he put the blame for everything on his long-suffering wife, by falsely accusing her of many things she had not and would not do or say. Naturally this hurt her very much and eventually she left him. In his loneliness, Oliver turned to drink and a few years later he died from sclerosis of the liver.

I see no point in summing up the above; the illustrations speak for themselves. However, my description of Oliver is not as over exaggerated as one might think. Although the Orphanage provided all the care and attention they could, there was not enough staff and time to give each child the love they should have and which is evident in most homes. This is proved by the following quote from a book that I read back in the 1980s entitled "The answer is in the Bible" written by a Christian Psychiatrist. "A person deprived of love in childhood, is prone to react aggressively against *imagined* wrongs." The accent is on 'imagined' as can be seen in the following that perhaps happens more often than we know.

When one partner is constantly bombarded with false accusations like confetti at a wedding, the one who is falsely accused, is very hurt, because they are unaware that the problem was lack of love in the other's childhood. The result is that however hard they try, it is IMPOSSIBLE for the accuser to believe their assurances that they would not do or say whatever they are accused of. This shows that events in childhood, both good and bad, affects everyone more than we realise. If couples were more open with each other regarding their lives before they met, this and perhaps other problems could be avoided. My advice to the recipient of these false accusations would be to ignore them and tactfully change the subject and stop wasting time trying to do the impossible - convince the other of their innocence. I know what I am talking about, for I have seen it happen.

I will conclude with the following quotes you might like to remember. "You always reap just what you sow, so do not plant the crop you have no wish to reap"

Here are two quotes from Ed Cole, a genuine American Evangelist, whom I have heard speaking several times. "Manhood and Christ likeness are synonymous"

"Being a male is a matter of birth, but Manhood is a matter of choice."

Do you not agree?

Freda Weaver

July 2008

Lightning Source UK Ltd.
Milton Keynes UK
16 August 2009

142695UK00001BA/2/P